Landscape Touch
Vol. 2

Sun Mi Kwon

ABOUT THIS BOOK

Welcome to a visual journey designed to inspire outdoor living possibilities. This book is crafted with the vision of empowering new homeowners to curate outdoor spaces that resonate with their lifestyle, while offering contractors and architects fresh perspectives and innovative ideas to elevate their craft, portfolios, and businesses. It serves as a valuable educational resource for students striving for excellence in their projects. With stunning and distinctive night views illuminated by captivating lighting designs, this book stands out as a unique treasure in its genre. Join us now as we explore the realm of endless possibilities. May this book guide you towards achieving your desired outdoor oasis. Whether you choose to implement the entire design or incorporate select elements, you'll find endless inspiration to enhance your outdoor living experience.

TABLE OF CONTENTS

House 2 - Day View

1	**2D HOUSE FLOOR PLAN**
2 - 12	**3D HOUSE & ISO VIEW**
13	**HOUSE FRONT & SIDE YARD VIEW**

14 - 17 **BACKYARD VIEW 1**
BBQ/Dining, herb garden, open
lattice wood patio cover, open lounge
& planters

18 - 29 **BACKYARD VIEW 2**
Pool, pool cabana, pool coping deck,
sun deck, spa, foot spa, spa lounge & planters
including accent dry rock garden

30 - 38 **BACKYARD VIEW 3**
Outdoor shower, jacuzzi, shower/jacuzzi lounge & planters

House 2 - Night View

39	**2D HOUSE FLOOR PLAN**
40 - 46	**3D HOUSE NIGHT VIEW**
47 - 52	**3D HOUSE ISO NIGHT VIEW**
53 - 54	**HOUSE FRONT & SIDE YARD NIGHT VIEW**

55 - 65 **BACKYARD VIEW 1**
BBQ/Dining, california room, herb garden w/vine trellis(wood or steel),
open lattice wood patio cover, open lounge & planters

66 - 75 **BACKYARD VIEW 2**
Pool : moon deck, cabana, coping deck lounge, lounge w/accent bench
& planters

76 - 84 **BACKYARD VIEW 3**
Entertainment lounge w/fire pit, outdoor shower, shower/jacuzzi lounge,
seating/lounge bench & planters including accent dry rock garden

Day View

2D FLOOR PLAN VIEW

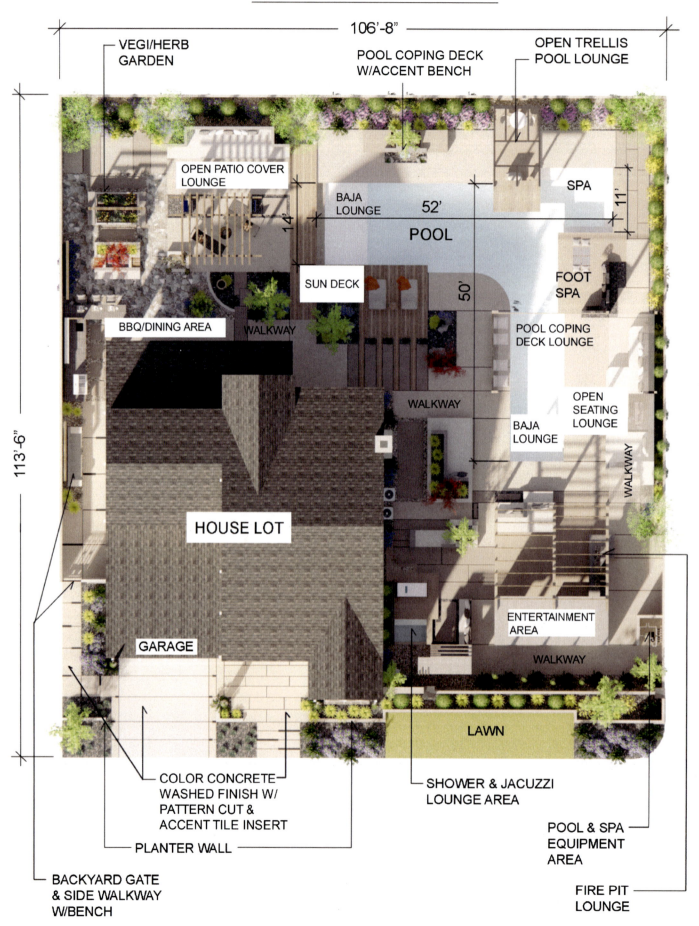

106'-8"

113'-6"

VEGI/HERB GARDEN

POOL COPING DECK W/ACCENT BENCH

OPEN TRELLIS POOL LOUNGE

OPEN PATIO COVER LOUNGE

SPA

BAJA LOUNGE

52'

POOL

11'

14'

SUN DECK

50'

FOOT SPA

WALKWAY

POOL COPING DECK LOUNGE

BBQ/DINING AREA

WALKWAY

OPEN SEATING LOUNGE

WALKWAY

BAJA LOUNGE

HOUSE LOT

WALKWAY

ENTERTAINMENT AREA

GARAGE

WALKWAY

LAWN

COLOR CONCRETE WASHED FINISH W/ PATTERN CUT & ACCENT TILE INSERT

SHOWER & JACUZZI LOUNGE AREA

PLANTER WALL

POOL & SPA EQUIPMENT AREA

BACKYARD GATE & SIDE WALKWAY W/BENCH

FIRE PIT LOUNGE

3D HOUSE VIEW 1

3D HOUSE VIEW 2

COLOR CONCRETE
WASHED FINISH W/
PATTERN CUT &
ACCENT TILE INSERT

PLANTER WALL

LAWN

POOL COPING DECK
W/ACCENT BENCH

CANTILEVER POOL CABANA DECK
W/OPEN PATIO COVER & SUNSHADE

SOLID CONCRETE ANCHOR COLUMN
FOR POOL LOUNGE SUNSHADE

POOL & SPA
EQUIPMENT
AREA

3D HOUSE VIEW 3

OUTDOOR SHOWER
& JACUZZI W/LOUNGE

OUTDOOR ENTERTAINMENT
LOUNGE W/FIRE PIT

OPEN LOUNGE BENCH
W/PLANTER BOX

OPEN SEATING &
FIRE PIT LOUNGE

WALKWAY

POOL
BAJA
SEATING

FOOT SPA LOUNGE
W/NATURAL STONE
SEAT BACKING

WALKWAY

POOL OPEN
SUN DECK

SPA

POOL

WALKWAY

CALIFONIA ROOM
W/DINING SET

BBQ & DINING

GARDEN LOUNGE
W/PLANTER BOX
& SEATING BENCH

HERB GARDEN
WOOD TRELLIS

WALKWAY

WALKWAY

HOUSE FRONT ISO VIEW

HOUSE RIGHT ISO VIEW

HOUSE RIGHT ISO VIEW

MAIN ENTRY

DRIVEWAY

WALKWAY

COLOR CONCRETE WASHED FINISH W/ PATTERN CUT & ACCENT TILE INSERT

SIDE ENTRY VIEW

BENCH W/ WOOD TRELLIS

SIDE ENTRY GATE

SMOOTH STUCCO FINISH WALL W/ACCENT NATURAL STONE PLAQUE

BBQ AREA

HOUSE LOT

BENCH

WATER FOUNTAIN/BIRD BATH

OPEN LATTICE WOOD PATIO COVER LOUNGE

TILE OR SLAB STONE AT COUNTER TOP

WOOD TRELLIS PANEL

SMOOTH STUCCO FINISH AT BACKSPLASH

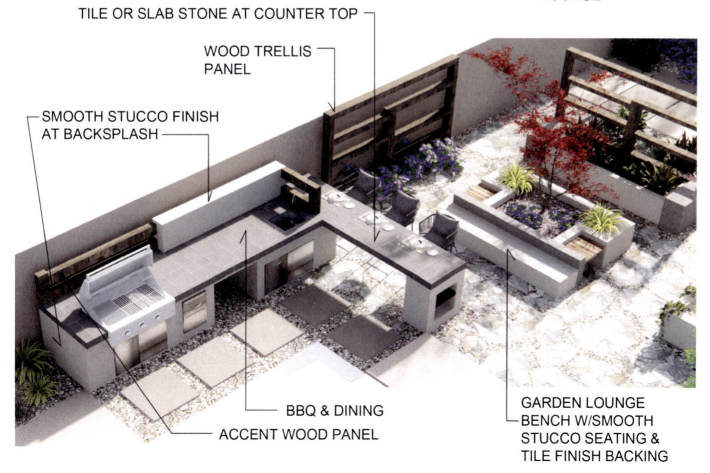

BBQ & DINING

ACCENT WOOD PANEL

GARDEN LOUNGE BENCH W/SMOOTH STUCCO SEATING & TILE FINISH BACKING

CALIFORNIA ROOM
W/DINING SET

BBQ DINING

BBQ & OPEN LOUNGE OVER VIEW

NATURAL STONE & DECORATIVE PEBBLE
AGGREGATE PAVING COMBO W/SAND GROUT

OUTDOOR VEGI/HERB GARDEN & BBQ /DINING AREA

SLAB STONE OR
TILE COUNTER TOP FINISH

SMOOTH STUCCO FINISH

OPEN LATTICE PATIO COVER & LOUNGE

OPTIONAL WATER FEATURE W/UNDERGROUND
WATER CATCH BASIN

OPEN PATIO COVER LOUNGE & POOL COPING DECK VIEW

POOL PATIO COVER & OPEN LOUNGE

POOL SUN DECK

POOL CABANA W/DAYBED

POOL COPING DECK W/ACCENT BENCH W/OPTIONAL WATER FEATURE

PORCELAIN TILE FINISH

NATURAL STONE FINISH

CANTILEVER POOL CABANA W/PATIO COVER

POOL & SUN DECK

SOLID CONCRETE ANCHOR COLUMNS FOR SUN SHADE CANOPY

SPA

LOUNGE

FOOT SPA
LOUNGE

POOL

SPA AREA LAYOUT

LOUNGE BENCH W/NATURAL STONE BACKING & FIRE PIT

FOOT SPA & LOUNGE LAYOUT

SPA & FOOT SPA W/LOUNGE DECK

SUN DECK W/DRY ROCK GARDEN

SPA & POOL COPING DECK LOUNGE VIEW

ENTERTAINMENT AREA

BACK TO BACK BENCH

FIRE PIT
LOUNGE BENCH

BENCH
W/PLANTER

POOL & ENTERTAINMENT AREA VIEW

SMOOTH STUCCO W/TILE FINISH BACKING

POOL BAJA
SEATING LOUNGE

ENTERTAINMENT AREA VIEW

STEEL FRAME OPEN PATIO COVER
W/POWDER COATED PAINT

CONCRETE WALL W/STONE
VENEER

ACCESS TO POOL EQUIPMENT AREA

OPEN LOUNGE BENCH & FIRE PIT

BACK TO BACK BENCH AT ENTERTAINMENT AREA

OUTDOOR THEATER AT ENTERTAINMENT AREA

OUTDOOR SHOWER & LOUNGE VIEWS

NATURAL STONE SHOWER WALL

BENCH

SHOWER AREA

DRY ROCK GARDEN

JACUZZI

PORCELAIN TILE

OVERSIZED PAVER

FIRE PIT & LOUNGE

OUTDOOR SHOWER & JACUZZI LOUNGE AREA

JACUZZI AREA W/DRY ROCK GARDEN

OPTIONAL WATER FEATURE
W/UNDERGROUND CATCH BASIN
AT DRY ROCK GARDEN AREA

Night View

2D FLOOR PLAN VIEW

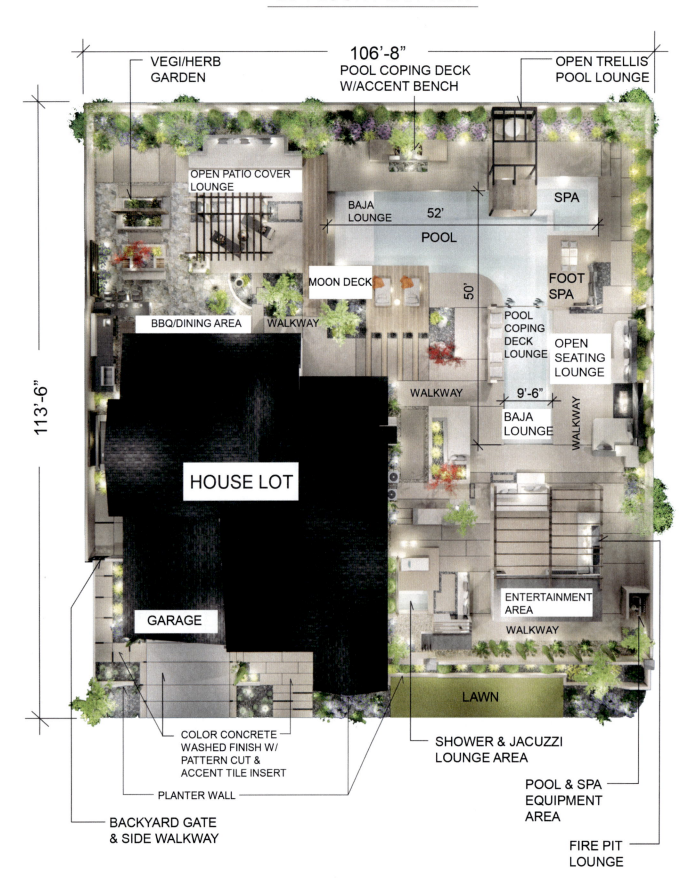

VEGI/HERB GARDEN

106'-8"
POOL COPING DECK W/ACCENT BENCH

OPEN TRELLIS POOL LOUNGE

OPEN PATIO COVER LOUNGE

BAJA LOUNGE

52'

SPA

POOL

MOON DECK

FOOT SPA

BBQ/DINING AREA

WALKWAY

50'

POOL COPING DECK LOUNGE

OPEN SEATING LOUNGE

113'-6"

WALKWAY

9'-6"

WALKWAY

BAJA LOUNGE

HOUSE LOT

ENTERTAINMENT AREA

WALKWAY

GARAGE

LAWN

COLOR CONCRETE WASHED FINISH W/ PATTERN CUT & ACCENT TILE INSERT

SHOWER & JACUZZI LOUNGE AREA

PLANTER WALL

POOL & SPA EQUIPMENT AREA

BACKYARD GATE & SIDE WALKWAY

FIRE PIT LOUNGE

3D HOUSE NIGHT VIEW 1

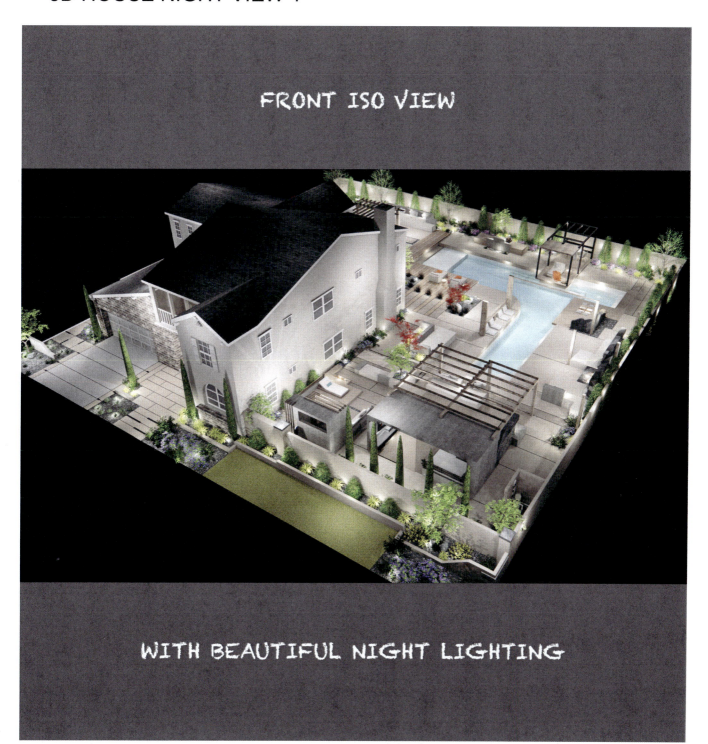

FRONT ISO VIEW

WITH BEAUTIFUL NIGHT LIGHTING

3D HOUSE NIGHT VIEW 2

DESIGNED PATTERN CUT WALKWAY

FOOT SPA LOUNGE W/NATURAL STONE SEAT BACKING

CANTILEVER POOL CABANA DECK W/OPEN PATIO & SUNSHADE

POOL OPEN MOON DECK

OPEN PATIO COVER LOUNGE

GARDEN LOUNGE W/PLANTER BOX & SEATING BENCH

DESIGNED PATTERN CUT WALKWAY

HERB GARDEN WOOD TRELLIS

SPA

POOL

BBQ & DINING

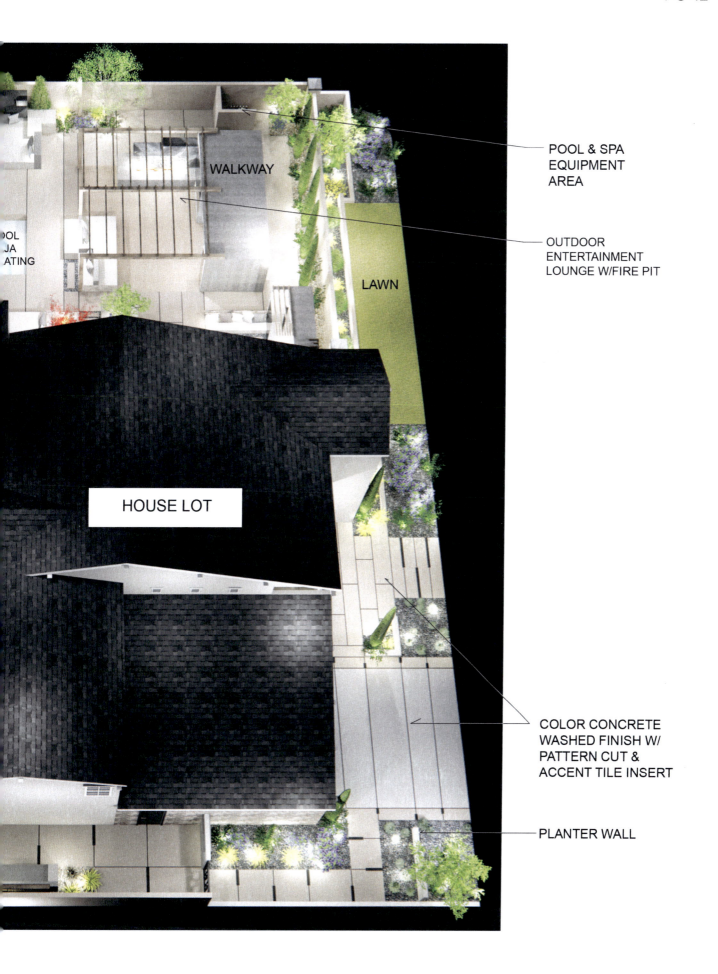

POOL & SPA
EQUIPMENT
AREA

OUTDOOR
ENTERTAINMENT
LOUNGE W/FIRE PIT

WALKWAY

LAWN

OOL
JA
ATING

HOUSE LOT

COLOR CONCRETE
WASHED FINISH W/
PATTERN CUT &
ACCENT TILE INSERT

PLANTER WALL

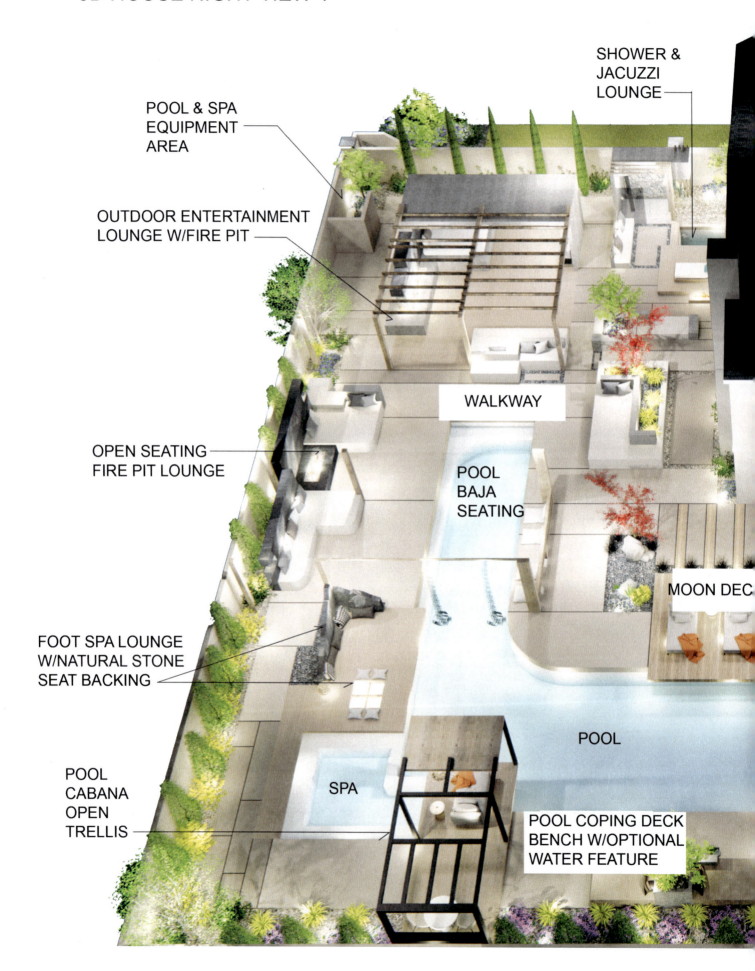

SHOWER & JACUZZI LOUNGE

POOL & SPA EQUIPMENT AREA

OUTDOOR ENTERTAINMENT LOUNGE W/FIRE PIT

WALKWAY

OPEN SEATING FIRE PIT LOUNGE

POOL BAJA SEATING

MOON DEC

FOOT SPA LOUNGE W/NATURAL STONE SEAT BACKING

POOL

POOL CABANA OPEN TRELLIS

SPA

POOL COPING DECK BENCH W/OPTIONAL WATER FEATURE

HOUSE LOT

SIDE WALKWAY
BENCH W/TRELLIS

BBQ & DINING

ACCENT WOOD
TRELLIS
ON THE SIDE

VEGI/HERB
PLANTER

OPEN PATIO COVER
LOUNGE

WALKWAY

3D HOUSE NIGHT VIEW 5

3D HOUSE NIGHT VIEW 6

HOUSE FRONT ISO NIGHT VIEW

HOUSE RIGHT ISO NIGHT VIEW

HOUSE LEFT ISO NIGHT VIEW

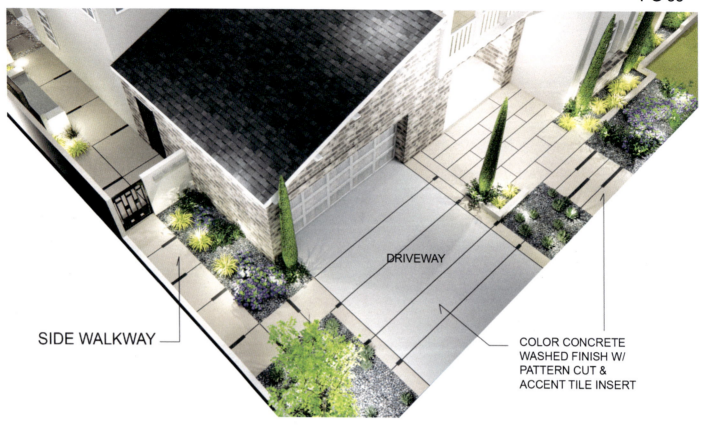

SIDE WALKWAY

DRIVEWAY

COLOR CONCRETE
WASHED FINISH W/
PATTERN CUT &
ACCENT TILE INSERT

WALKWAY TO SIDE GATE

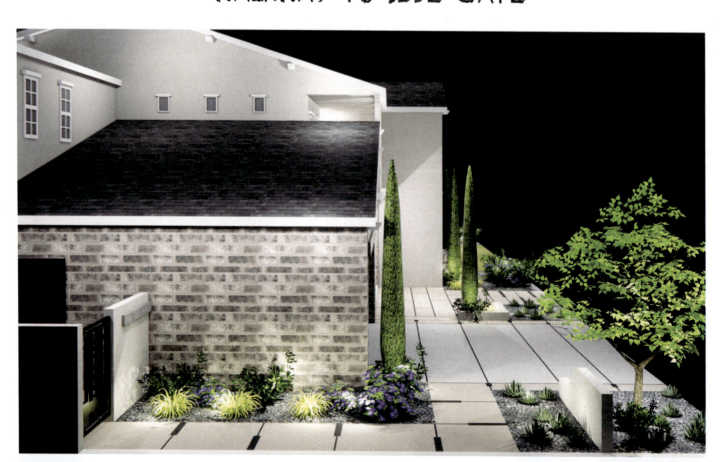

BENCH W/ WOOD TRELLIS

NEW WROUGHT IRON GATE

COLOR CONCRETE WASHED FINISH W/PATTERN CUT
& ACCENT TILE INSERT

BBQ AREA

SOLID CONCRETE W/AGGREGATE
OR LOOSE PEBBLE

DINING AREA

OPTIONAL WATER FEATURE
W/UNDERGROUND WATER CATCH BASIN

NATURAL STONE PAVING W/AGGREGATE PEBBLE INSERT

BBQ & DINING NEXT TO CALIFORNIA ROOM

OPEN LOUNGE W/ PATIO COVER

OPEN LOUNGE W/PATIO COVER NEXT TO HERB GARDEN

NATURAL STONE PAVING W/EMBEDDED PEBBLE GROUT

NATURAL STONE /OR/PORCELAIN TILE VENEER FINISH ⌐

⌐ SMOOTH STUCCO FINISH

VEGI/HERB GARDEN

POWDER COATED STEEL FRAME ACCENT VINE TRELLIS ⌐

OPTIONAL WATER FEATURE W/UNDERGROUND
WATER CATCH BASIN

SOLID CONCRETE COLUMN W/WOOD PLANK LOOK

OPEN LATTICE PATIO COVER AT OPEN LOUNGE

OPEN PATIO LOUNGE OVER VIEW

OPEN PATIO COVER VIEW

BBQ & DINING & OPEN LOUNGE AREA VIEW

OPEN LOUNGE AREA BENCH

OPEN LOUNGE & HERB GARDEN LAYOUT

BEAUTIFUL NIGHT LOUNGE VIEW

MOON DECK BY THE POOL

BAJA LOUNGE W/POOL ACCESS

MOON DECK

POOL COPING DECK W/ACCENT BENCH

OPTIONAL
WATER FEATURE
W/UNDERGROUND
WATER CATCH BASIN

POOL CABANA

POOL COPING DECK LOUNGE & POOL CABANA

CANTILEVER POOL CABANA

POWDER COATED STEEL FRAME

NIGHT VIEW
AT POOL & SPA

NATURAL STONE OR PORCELAIN TILE FINISH AT
SPA & POOL CABANA DECK

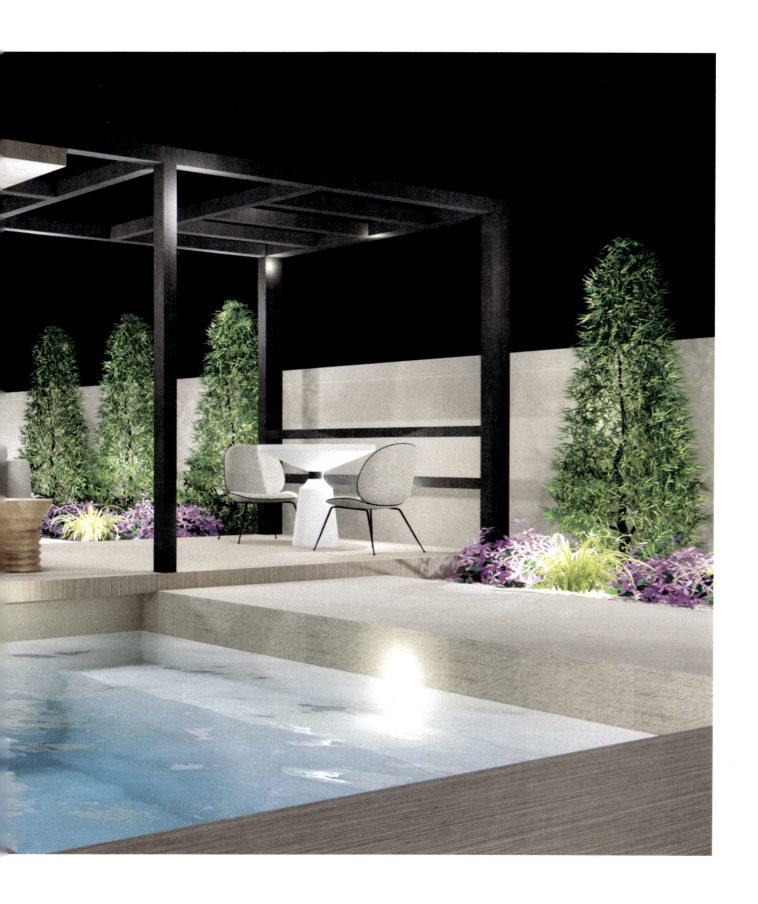

FOOT SPA
SEATING DECK LOUNGE
W/NATURAL STONE BACKING

4 PERSON
FOOT SPA
W/WATER JET

SPA

POOL

OPEN SEATING LOUNGE POOL DECK W/FIRE PIT

SMOOTH STUCCO FINISH SEATING

NATURAL STONE OR MANUFACTURAL SLAB
STONE FINISH FIRE PIT & BACKING WALL

SOLID CONCRETE COLUMN

POWDER COATED STEEL FRAME BACKING

POOL COPING DECK SEATING W/RAIL BACKING

WASHED FINISH CONCRETE
POOL COPING
& DECK W/PATTERN CUT

ENTERTAINMENT PATIO COVER LOUNGE &
POOL COPING DECK LAYOUT

POOL BAJA SEATING

POOL DECK
BENCH
W/PLANTER

SMOOTH STUCCO SEATING

NATURAL STONE OR PORCELAIN
TILE BACKING

EMBEDDED OR LOOSE PEBBLE BAND

ENTERTAINMENT AREA DAYBED W/FIRE PIT & BACK TO BACK BENCH

POOL EQUIPMENT
ACCESS WALKWAY

OUTDOOR SCREEN THEATER

JACUZZI
LOUNGE DECK

SHOWER & JACUZZI LOUNGE W/FIRE PIT

POWDER COADTED STEEL FRAME

NATURAL STONE OR PORCELAIN TILE

STONE ACCENT SHOWER WALL

OPTIONAL WATER FEATURE AT ACCENT DRY ROCK GARDEN
W/UNDERGROUND WATER CATCH BASIN

JACUZZI

DRY ROCK GARDEN

SHOWER & JACUZZI LOUNGE LAYOUT

OPEN BENCH
LOUNGE AREA

MY FAVORITE NIGHT HANG OUT

ABOUT THE AUTHOR

Sun Mi Kwon brings over 23 years of experience as a living space and landscape designer, enriched by extensive hands-on expertise. With a robust background in on-site work, she possesses a deep understanding of practical landscape design principles. Throughout her career, Sun Mi has collaborated with a wide spectrum of clients, including private individuals, industry-independent contractors, and architects. Collectively, her contributions have led to the creation of over 1000 unique designs, showcasing her versatility and innovation in the field.

Made in the USA
Las Vegas, NV
28 July 2024

93089777R00057